NICARAGUA'S DEMOCRATIC COLLAPSE

HEARING

BEFORE THE

SUBCOMMITTEE ON
THE WESTERN HEMISPHERE

OF THE

COMMITTEE ON FOREIGN AFFAIRS
HOUSE OF REPRESENTATIVES

ONE HUNDRED FOURTEENTH CONGRESS

SECOND SESSION

SEPTEMBER 15, 2016

Serial No. 114–235

Printed for the use of the Committee on Foreign Affairs

Available via the World Wide Web: http://www.foreignaffairs.house.gov/ or
http://www.gpo.gov/fdsys/

U.S. GOVERNMENT PUBLISHING OFFICE

21–546PDF   WASHINGTON : 2016

For sale by the Superintendent of Documents, U.S. Government Publishing Office
Internet: bookstore.gpo.gov   Phone: toll free (866) 512–1800; DC area (202) 512–1800
Fax: (202) 512–2104   Mail: Stop IDCC, Washington, DC 20402–0001

COMMITTEE ON FOREIGN AFFAIRS

EDWARD R. ROYCE, California, *Chairman*

CHRISTOPHER H. SMITH, New Jersey
ILEANA ROS-LEHTINEN, Florida
DANA ROHRABACHER, California
STEVE CHABOT, Ohio
JOE WILSON, South Carolina
MICHAEL T. McCAUL, Texas
TED POE, Texas
MATT SALMON, Arizona
DARRELL E. ISSA, California
TOM MARINO, Pennsylvania
JEFF DUNCAN, South Carolina
MO BROOKS, Alabama
PAUL COOK, California
RANDY K. WEBER SR., Texas
SCOTT PERRY, Pennsylvania
RON DeSANTIS, Florida
MARK MEADOWS, North Carolina
TED S. YOHO, Florida
CURT CLAWSON, Florida
SCOTT DesJARLAIS, Tennessee
REID J. RIBBLE, Wisconsin
DAVID A. TROTT, Michigan
LEE M. ZELDIN, New York
DANIEL DONOVAN, New York

ELIOT L. ENGEL, New York
BRAD SHERMAN, California
GREGORY W. MEEKS, New York
ALBIO SIRES, New Jersey
GERALD E. CONNOLLY, Virginia
THEODORE E. DEUTCH, Florida
BRIAN HIGGINS, New York
KAREN BASS, California
WILLIAM KEATING, Massachusetts
DAVID CICILLINE, Rhode Island
ALAN GRAYSON, Florida
AMI BERA, California
ALAN S. LOWENTHAL, California
GRACE MENG, New York
LOIS FRANKEL, Florida
TULSI GABBARD, Hawaii
JOAQUIN CASTRO, Texas
ROBIN L. KELLY, Illinois
BRENDAN F. BOYLE, Pennsylvania

AMY PORTER, *Chief of Staff*   THOMAS SHEEHY, *Staff Director*
JASON STEINBAUM, *Democratic Staff Director*

————

SUBCOMMITTEE ON THE WESTERN HEMISPHERE

JEFF DUNCAN, South Carolina, *Chairman*

CHRISTOPHER H. SMITH, New Jersey
ILEANA ROS-LEHTINEN, Florida
MICHAEL T. McCAUL, Texas
MATT SALMON, Arizona
RON DeSANTIS, Florida
TED S. YOHO, Florida
DANIEL DONOVAN, New York

ALBIO SIRES, New Jersey
JOAQUIN CASTRO, Texas
ROBIN L. KELLY, Illinois
GREGORY W. MEEKS, New York
ALAN GRAYSON, Florida
ALAN S. LOWENTHAL, California

(II)

CONTENTS

NICARAGUA'S DEMOCRATIC COLLAPSE

THURSDAY, SEPTEMBER 15, 2016

House of Representatives,
Subcommittee on the Western Hemisphere,
Committee on Foreign Affairs,
Washington, DC.

The committee met, pursuant to notice, at 10:00 a.m., in room 2172 Rayburn House Office Building, Hon. Jeff Duncan (chairman of the subcommittee) presiding.

Mr. DUNCAN. A quorum being present, the subcommittee will come to order. I would now like to recognize myself for an opening statement on the hearing Nicaragua's Democratic Collapse.

We meet today to register our deep concern over the collapse of democracy in Nicaragua and conduct oversight of the Obama administration's priorities in the country, in view of U.S. interests and recent events.

While Nicaragua does not suffer the same problems with citizen security, gang wars, or migration to the United States as the Northern Triangle countries have experienced, it is the poorest Central American country and second poorest in the Western Hemisphere, only after Haiti.

Under President Ortega's multiple terms as President, he has taken increasingly blatant steps to concentrate political power into a single party FSLN-ruled system controlling the majority at executive, legislative, judicial, and electoral branches of government. In 2011, 2012, 2014 elections, the State Department and other observers found fraud and other major irregularities had occurred. Since then, the State Department has documented in several reports that Nicaraguan Government agents have committed arbitrary or unlawful killings, used excessive force and torture in prisons, and limited the Nicaraguan people's freedom of speech, religion, and the press.

Compounding these problems, in 2014 the FSLN-dominated National Assembly passed 97 constitutional amendments and Ortega pushed through a new military code and reform of the National Police, giving Ortega more political control over the country. Ortega also appointed his sons and daughters positions of Ambassador, Presidential advisor, and his wife holds the post of communication minister, government spokesperson and now is a Vice Presidential pick ahead of the November 6 elections, even though Nicaragua's Constitution bars those related to the President from being a candidate for Vice President.

In June, the Supreme Court stripped the opposition Independent Liberal Party, PLI, and the Citizen Action Party, PAC, of their chosen leaders.

In July, the Supreme Electoral Council removed 28 PLI National Assembly members from their democratically elected positions. Ortega has even announced that no international election observers will be allowed for the November election, despite the wishes of the Nicaraguan civil society. Such an erosion of democracy and freedom and utter disregard for the rule of law and human rights should elicit cries of outrage from democratic countries in Latin America, and the Caribbean, and from the Obama administration. Yet, while a few countries have made statements and the OAS, Organization of American States, and Human Rights Foundation have expressed concerns, nothing more has happened.

Today, there appears to be no cost to Ortega for undermining democracy and the rule of law in the pursuit of his own personal interests.

The United States has national interests at stake in Nicaragua and Central America. Nicaragua is a member of the Central American Free Trade Agreement, CAFTA-DR, thus, benefitting from access to U.S. markets. There are multiple U.S. businesses operating in the country, 177 Peace Corps volunteers reflecting the U.S. spirit of compassion, and many U.S. citizens have chosen to retire there.

Strategically, Nicaragua occupies the geographic center of Central America and is, therefore, key not only for legitimate commerce but also for drugs, contraband goods, migrant flows, and potential security challenges to the Northern Hemisphere. That said, we want to see a stable, prosperous Nicaragua that adheres to democratic principles, respects the rule of law and separation of powers, supports human rights, and responds to the will of the Nicaraguan people. We want to see that Nicaragua and all Central America achieve greater security and economic growth, limit migration north to the United States, and minimize the strategic influence of actors like China, Russia, and Iran from establishing a greater presence in the region. Unfortunately, under Ortega's tenure just the opposite is occurring.

Furthermore, Ortega has displayed clear contempt for the common accepted principles of government-to-government relations with the United States through the expulsion of three U.S. citizens traveling on official U.S. business in June from the country. This follows the expulsion of Freedom House's Latin American programs director and students from Mexico National Autonomous University earlier this year.

Ortega has also continued to pursue deeper relations with China through the Inter-Oceanic Canal Project, even though there appears to be limited progress on this canal and tremendous public opposition to his construction, Ortega has given the Hong Kong-based company HKND enormous discretion in building and operating the canal. Moreover, Russia has also been building stronger military ties to Nicaragua. Russia recently sold 50 T-72 tanks to Nicaragua, established and is expanding a large law enforcement training center in Managua, and gained access to Nicaragua's air space and ports.

Iran has also continued courting Nicaragua, sporadically pursuing interest in Nicaraguan ports during the last decade, a strong diplomatic presence, and student exchanges with Iranian religious schools. Iran's continuing interest in Nicaragua was highlighted by a visit last month by Iranian Foreign Minister Zarif, where Zarif expressed interest in collaborating with Nicaragua on the Inter-Oceanic Canal and extending economic energy and trade ties.

So, given the U.S. interest in Asia, the Middle East, and Europe, I am left wondering what the Obama administration is doing to understand and respond to the strategic implications of these countries' overtures to Nicaragua and to reassure our friends in the region, such as Costa Rica and Colombia, that we have particular concerns with Nicaragua's expanding military relationship with Russia.

The State Department's fiscal year 2017 budget requests included over $14 million for Nicaragua. Although I support providing assistance to promote U.S. interests, given the current landscape in Nicaragua, I am deeply skeptical as to the effectiveness of the administration's priorities and efforts in the country. After all, the situation looks very bleak ahead of the November elections.

If Ortega continues with his current activities, perhaps instead it is a time for the administration to consider a re-think of its constructive engagement policy toward Nicaragua. To that end, what has the current U.S. policy achieved? Is Nicaragua more or less democratic? To what degree has the administration's policy help dissuade Nicaragua from pursuing partnerships with countries like Iran and Russia that potentially threaten U.S. interest in the region? If things do not change before the election, I believe the State Department should very strongly consider sanctions denying Nicaragua the benefits of CAFTA-DR and work with the Treasury Department to vote against loans in the international lending institutions until the Government of Nicaragua takes steps to respect freedom, fair and open elections, democracy, and the rule of law.

So with that, I will turn to the ranking member for his opening statement.

Mr. Sires. Thank you, Mr. Chairman, for holding this hearing and thank you to our witnesses who have joined us here today.

Since winning the presidency a decade ago, Daniel Ortega has pursued a goal of gaining absolute political control over Nicaraguan society. With the November 6th Presidential election in Nicaragua approaching, and with his control over all the nation's public institutions, Ortega is poised to win his third consecutive term, this time with his wife serving as his running mate.

How has Ortega been able to concentrate his power? Not satisfied with simply winning an election widely deemed fraudulent in 2006 and 2011, as President, Ortega has used his influence to gain control over the courts, rescind Presidential term limits, disqualify opposition leaders from running for office, remove opposition lawmakers from the National Assembly, and ban international election observers from the country.

The opposition party including the largest, PLI, Independent Liberal Party, are fractured and in no position to effectively confront Ortega's overwhelming political power and influence. Both the Obama administration and Congress have expressed grave concerns over Ortega's blatant, undemocratic power grab, as well as his expulsion of the opposition legislators and U.S. citizens.

Earlier this year, Ortega's Government needlessly expelled an American scholar from the American War College doing research on the supposed Nicaragua Canal. Additionally, they have also expelled two U.S. Embassy officials without cause and routinely harassed American visitors traveling down to Nicaragua.

Congress and the administration need to work together and find ways to empower the Nicaraguan people and counteract Ortega's hostile behavior toward innocent civilians. That is why I was proud to work with my good friend from Florida, Congresswoman Ros-Lehtinen and our Chairman Duncan, among several other colleagues from both sides of the aisle to introduce and pass H.R. 5708, the Nicaragua Investment Conditionality Act, NICA.

H.R. 5708 calls on the U.S. Government to oppose loans at international financial institutions for Nicaragua, unless the Nicaraguan Government takes effective steps to hold free, fair, and transparent elections and commits to upholding democratic principle. It is my hope that this legislation will pass the Senate and quickly be signed into law by President Obama.

I look forward to hearing from our witnesses their points of view regarding the current situation in Nicaragua and how the U.S. and the international community can effectively respond to the nondemocratic actions of Daniel Ortega.

Thank you.

Mr. DUNCAN. The Chairman will now recognize the former chairwoman of the full committee and now chairwoman of the Subcommittee on Africa and the Middle East—or Middle East and North Africa, I guess is what is called. Isn't that right?

Ms. ROS-LEHTINEN. I will take that.

Mr. DUNCAN. You are recognized for 5 minutes.

Ms. ROS-LEHTINEN. Thank you, Mr. Chairman. And that beard looks pretty sexy on you.

Mr. DUNCAN. Well, thank you.

Ms. ROS-LEHTINEN. I like it.

Thank you for holding this hearing, Mr. Chairman. I think it is so important for your subcommittee to shine a spotlight on Nicaragua and the abusive actions orchestrated by Daniel Ortega and his decrepit regime. You have described them. The ranking member Albio Sires, has described them. We all know it.

And on December 1, 2011, when I was chair of the Foreign Affairs Committee, I held a hearing on elections in Nicaragua. And now here we are, 5 years later, nada has changed.

In February 2016, Ortega detained and expelled Freedom House Latin America Director Dr. Carlos Ponce. And in June 2016, Ortega expelled three United States Government officials.

Ortega has also forced the Nicaraguan Supreme Court to not recognize the leaders of two opposition political parties. He has even removed 28 opposition deputies and alternates from the National Assembly without any due process and in the most undemocratic way possible. Then, he chose his wife to be his running mate in the upcoming illegitimate elections in an effort to extend the Ortega dynasty at the expense of the people.

We have seen Ortega send his cronies to break up peaceful marches by Nicaraguan civil society and peaceful protestors who are simply calling for inclusive elections to be observed by international and domestic experts.

If these problems sound familiar to you, Mr. Chairman, it is because we have seen these deplorable acts in the Western Hemisphere just a bit too often. Ortega has taken a page out of the Maduro and Castro playbook on how to silence the opposition and maintain a grip on power. And while the failed policies toward Cuba and Venezuela tend to grab the headlines, we cannot forget about the other rogue regimes in the region like Nicaragua that subvert democratic principles.

What is it going to take for us to take action? Russian tanks are in Nicaragua. What do we think they are going to be used for? Of course, it is going to be scare and intimidate the public, just like the National Police and the military is being used by Ortega to abuse the people and violate their human rights, as we speak. We cannot give Ortega a free pass on these actions.

I know that State Department officials will say that at least Nicaragua is cooperating with the U.S. on counter-narcotics operations, but the truth is cooperation is very limited and it is designed to detract our attention away from its bad actions. These rogue regimes in the region know how to play us like a violin. Bad actors in the region understand that as long as they can cooperate, even under a limited basis with U.S. authorities on counter-narcotics, then we typically turn the other way when it comes to democracy and human rights. This charade must not be allowed to continue. We have got to start holding Ortega and his ilk accountable.

And thank you, Mr. Chairman, for the markup earlier. I am honored to be the Republican lead, alongside my good friend Debbie Wasserman Schultz, in introducing H.R. 851. Thank you for its passage. This resolution, as you pointed out, expresses the profound concern of Congress about the ongoing political, economic, social, and humanitarian crisis in Venezuela. It calls for the release of all political prisoners, for Venezuelan officials to respect constitutional and democratic process. As we know, the economic situation continues to deteriorate. Inflation has caused high food prices, making it difficult for people to afford even the most basic necessities.

Also, Maduro continues to unjustly detain Venezuelan political prisoners from the opposition. The regime is even extrajudicially holding American citizens.

So, I think you for the markup on that resolution and I thank you for the markup for supporting the Nicaraguan Investment Conditionality Act, a bill that I am proud to have introduced with the ranking member of your subcommittee, Mr. Sires, as well as the chairman of our subcommittee, Mr. Duncan.

Taking his cues from Ortega and seeing the tepid response from the international community, Ortega has ignored the Nicaraguan Constitution, manipulated the nation's Supreme Court and its Electoral Council to empower his regime and silence his opposition.

So, I thank you for the markup and the passage of this resolution to say that they have got to hold free, fair, and transparent elections, promote democracy, strengthen the rule of law, respect the right of freedom of association or they don't get these loans from the United States and the international community.

Thank you so much, Mr. Chairman.

Mr. DUNCAN. And you got all that done in just 4 seconds over your time. Thanks for the comment on the beard. I don't know how long it will stay.

And we can all take a page out of your playbook for leadership on issues with regard to Latin American. So, thank you for that. Congratulations on passage of that.

Ms. ROS-LEHTINEN. Thank you.

Mr. DUNCAN. The Chair will now recognize Mr. Castro for an opening statement.

Mr. CASTRO. Thank you, Chairman, and thank you for holding this hearing today.

The United States has an interest in making sure that around the world, particularly with allied nations, human rights and democracy are respected, whether their leaders fall on the right side of the spectrum or the left side of the spectrum, whether they are liberal, or conservative, or communists, or fascists, making sure that these nations have leaders who respect their people. That means respecting the institutions of democracy. And what we have seen in Nicaragua is especially troubling.

And so, I look forward to the testimony and thank you for holding the hearing. I yield back.

Mr. DUNCAN. I thank the member. No other member seeking recognition. We will go ahead and start the hearing.

Before I recognize the witnesses, there is a lighting system in front of you. Just try to adhere to 5 minutes. We are not really pressed today, other than members are trying to get out of town for their weekend, back in the District, campaigning, and other things. So, if we can just stay on time, that would be great.

Bios were provided to the members. So, I am not going to read the bios.

Welcome again. I think I know Mr. Gonzalez has been here before and I welcome the young lady. So, I am going to recognize you in order. Mr. Gonzalez, you are recognized for 5 minutes.

STATEMENT OF MR. JUAN GONZALEZ, DEPUTY ASSISTANT SECRETARY, BUREAU OF WESTERN HEMISPHERE AFFAIRS, U.S. DEPARTMENT OF STATE

Mr. GONZALEZ. Thank you, Mr. Chairman, ranking members, and members of the committee. It is an honor to testify before you today. I have submitted my testimony for the record and I thought, with your concurrence, I would use my time just to highlight the main points.

Mr. DUNCAN. Can you pull that microphone just a little bit closer? We are trying to record all of this for posterity.

Mr. GONZALEZ. Understood. Without your objection, Mr. Chairman, I would like to submit my testimony for the record and just highlight the main points in my opening remarks.

I last testified, as you mentioned, when this committee held a hearing on border security in March, which remains an incredibly issue and a national security priority for the administration. And thank you for your leadership in chairing that hearing.

And I cannot let an opportunity go by to also thank this committee for its support for Central America. To be frank, we would be nowhere without you and we are actually very working aggressively to implement the U.S. strategy for engagement in Central America and it is all thanks to the work of this committee and the Members of Congress.

Today we also celebrate the 195th anniversary of Central America's independence. The region's history is closely intertwined with ours and the region's prosperity and security has always mattered to the United States. Throughout, we have seen positive signs, like the region's active efforts to integrate and cement trade partnerships with the United States, Europe, Asia but challenges abound as well. Corruption is rampant throughout. Transnational criminal organizations challenge the state in some areas.

Equally concerning is the state of democratic institutions in various parts of Central America but I would say most so in Nicaragua, where President Daniel Ortega has been working to transform the country into a de facto one-party system.

The government's recent actions restrict free and fair elections and to dismantle democratic institutions, such as independent political parties are troubling to us. While certain freedoms continue to exist and elections are still being held in November, the Sandinista National Liberal Front has applied the tools of incumbency, influenced the judiciary, and manipulated the political influence and intimidation to eliminate the system of checks and balances necessary for a vibrant and functioning democracy. The cumulative effect of these actions threatens to render the upcoming elections a pantomime of democracy.

And the question before us is how to respond. In sum, the approach we are taking if four-fold. First, we are voicing our concerns and exposing such authoritarian actions for what they are. To avoid bilateralizing the issue, we need to work with multi-lateral organizations and we are doing this.

Second, we are standing in solidarity with Nicaraguan civil society and supporting democratic institutions in every way we can. To be clear, ours is not an anti-Ortega strategy; it is a pro-Nicaragua strategy and we are working with the opposition, as well as elements of the Sandinistas.

Third, we are engaging directly with the Nicaraguan people. The future of Nicaragua will not be determined in Washington and only by the Nicaraguan people. So, our Ambassador is out there every day making the case for better U.S.-Nicaraguan relations and speaking on behalf of strong democratic institutions. Actually, I don't think Ambassador Laura Dogu sleeps. She is an active advocate on behalf of the United States.

And fourth, we continue to have interests in the country and we need to continue advancing those interests. So, we will continue to cooperate with them in areas where we have a direct interest, like counter-narcotics and combating transnational criminal organizations.

Again, we continue to closely monitor the developments as they relate to the election. It is something incredibly concerning. And we look forward to working with members of this committee on the best ways to promote our interest in Nicaragua. Thank you very much.

[The prepared statement of Mr. Gonzalez follows:]

TESTIMONY OF
JUAN S. GONZALEZ
DEPUTY ASSISTANT SECRETARY OF STATE
BUREAU OF WESTERN HEMISPHERE AFFAIRS
U.S. DEPARTMENT OF STATE
BEFORE
THE SUBCOMMITTEE ON WESTERN HEMISPHERE
HOUSE COMMITTEE ON FOREIGN AFFAIRS
SEPTEMBER 15, 2016

Chairman Duncan, Ranking Member Sires, and Members of the Committee:

Thank you for the opportunity to testify before you today. Today's hearing coincides with the 195th anniversary of Central American independence and provides an opportunity to review the evolution of U.S. policy toward the region. Our policy seeks to promote a region that is secure, prosperous, and democratic, and thanks to bipartisan support of the U.S. Congress, we are investing significant resources toward this end. But we also see troubling signals with regard to democratic space in Nicaragua that may have important regional implications.

We are at a critical juncture in the U.S.-Nicaragua bilateral relationship. While the Nicaraguan government engages with us on some issues, and remains a willing partner in countering irregular migration and drug trafficking, there is no question that since taking office in 2006, Nicaraguan President Daniel Ortega has been working to transform the country into a de facto one-party system. Its recent actions to restrict free and fair elections and to dismantle democratic institutions, such as independent political parties, are troubling. While certain freedoms continue to exist and elections are still being held, the Sandinista National Liberation Front (FSLN) has applied the tools of government, the judiciary, political manipulation, and intimidation to eliminate the system of checks and balances necessary for a vibrant and functioning democracy.

The United States is concerned by the actions of the Nicaraguan government and Supreme Court to limit democratic space in advance of presidential and legislative elections in November. The cumulative effect of these actions threatens to render the upcoming elections a pantomime of democracy. We strongly urge the Nicaraguan government to change course and create a more open environment for free and fair elections that will allow the Nicaraguan people to determine the future of their country, and to restore opposition political parties to the control of their members. We support Nicaraguan civil society, business leaders, and religious leaders' efforts to continue to advocate for a strengthening of democratic institutions, a separation of powers, and a fair electoral process.

I want to highlight recent actions taken by the Nicaraguan government to shrink the democratic space in the lead-up to the November 2016 presidential and legislative elections.

- President Daniel Ortega announced June 4 that international election observers would not be allowed to monitor the upcoming elections.

- On June 8, the Nicaraguan Supreme Court stripped the opposition Independent Liberal Party (PLI) of its long-time leader, Eduardo Montealegre. The Supreme Court designated a new leader who is widely considered to be beholden the FSLN.

- The Supreme Court took similar action June 17 when it invalidated the leadership of the Citizen Action Party, the only remaining opposition party with the legal standing to present a presidential candidate.

- As a result of these decisions, all Municipal Electoral Councils, which determine voting procedures and monitor votes on election day, consist only of members or allies of the FSLN.

- On July 29, at the request of the new PLI leader, the Supreme Electoral Council removed 28 PLI national assembly members from their popularly-elected positions.

- On August 2, Ortega named First Lady Rosario Murillo as his running mate. Murillo has been running day-to-day government activities for several years and serves as spokesperson.

- President Ortega is able to run for his third term due to a constitutional reform passed in 2014 after the FSLN gained a super majority in the National Assembly in the 2011 elections that international and domestic observers characterized as seriously flawed.

- The State Department's 2015 Human Rights Report documents a number of additional actions that the Nicaraguan government has taken to limit free and fair elections. For example: making party membership mandatory for many public sector employees and requiring non-FSLN members to present government-issued identification cards in order to vote.

We have spoken out against these developments in public and private, both in the United States and in Nicaragua, and are working to internationalize the response via the UN, OAS, EU, and like-minded democracies.

Our mission with respect to Nicaragua is to promote a prosperous, secure, and democratic Nicaragua that is an integrated and constructive bilateral, regional, and global actor. As such, we focus our engagement with Nicaragua on three pillars – prosperity, security, and democracy.

The U.S. Strategy for Engagement in Central America, including Nicaragua, focuses on three overarching lines of action: 1) promoting prosperity and regional economic integration, 2) enhancing security, and 3) promoting improved governance. U.S. foreign assistance for Nicaragua advances these focus areas by working with civil society to prevent the erosion of national democratic governance, improve citizen security along Nicaragua's Caribbean coast and in the Northern regions, and support efforts to reduce the transshipment of drugs through Nicaragua. Our assistance programs are primarily directed at civil society, in order to limit engagement with the central government.

Nicaragua has avoided the gang and drug-related violence that plagues some of its neighbors. Nicaragua also remains focused on denying entry to northbound irregular migrants and has resisted domestic and international pressure from countries to the south to allow these groups free passage. Because Nicaragua is the second poorest country in the hemisphere, it is important that we maintain our robust trade and economic relationship with Nicaragua, which benefits the Nicaraguan people and provides opportunities to American businesses. This includes strengthening the investment and business climate, improving agricultural productivity, and increasing access to education and workforce development through food for education, English-language, and technical training programs. U.S. exports to Nicaragua increased 18 percent from January–July 2016 compared with the same time period the previous year. The United States is now on pace to export approximately $200 million in oil products to Nicaragua in 2016, five times the amount exported in 2014.

Russia is Nicaragua's security partner of choice. We share Congressional concerns about Russian activities around the world. We are closely monitoring Russia's presence in Nicaragua.

Going forward, we will also remain focused on the full range of our strategic interests with respect to Nicaragua. These interests will require, appropriately calibrated engagement with the Nicaraguan government. At the same time, our support for the right of the Nicaraguan people to exercise their fundamental freedoms and to choose their leadership in free and fair elections is unwavering; however, we will continue to articulate our objections to the actions the Nicaraguan government has taken to limit the democratic space in the lead-up to the November 2016 elections. We will vocalize our position bilaterally, and we will work together with our many partners in multilateral fora to underscore our support for Nicaraguan democracy. It is in the U.S. national interest to maintain engagement in areas that promote a prosperous, secure, and democratic Nicaragua so that the Nicaraguan people can be empowered to embrace freedom and their universal human rights.

I look forward to your questions.

Mr. DUNCAN. Thank you, Mr. Gonzalez.

Now, I will recognize the Honorable Marcela Escobari for 5 minutes.

STATEMENT OF THE HONORABLE MARCELA ESCOBARI, ASSISTANT ADMINISTRATOR, BUREAU FOR LATIN AMERICA AND THE CARIBBEAN, U.S. AGENCY FOR INTERNATIONAL DEVELOPMENT

Ms. ESCOBARI. Chairman Duncan and Ranking Member Sires, and members of the subcommittee, thank you for the opportunity to testify before you today and for speaking out on the Government of Nicaragua's efforts to restrict democracy.

I am grateful for the committee's support for the work of USAID and for your leadership in our engagement in Central America. I have actually just come back from the Northern Triangle and I saw firsthand how our support is making a difference. This is a historic opportunity to help these countries in their effort to improve the lives of their citizens and the political will for reform is definitely there.

Despite significant challenges, citizens are demanding accountability and local institutions are responding from CICIG in Guatemala to the show of independence in the Attorney General offices of each of these three countries, they are making significant strides in accountability and transparency.

These gains are in stark contrast to the situation in Nicaragua, where the Ortega administration continues to close democratic space and consolidate power. Nicaragua is the second poorest nation in the Western Hemisphere. The country has yet to reach the levels of income per capita it had in 1978. Criminal activities and violence are on the rise on the country's Caribbean coast, which is also the area with the worst poverty indicators, where 40 percent of boys and girls do not attend school. This is not a country that can afford a government that refuses to be held accountable and respond to those most in need of assistance.

We must continue to support the people of Nicaragua in their efforts to participate in the democratic process. And two-thirds of USAID's bilateral assistance focuses on this priority. We are supporting over 60 civil society organizations to help them be effective in advocating for citizens' rights. We are also helping nurture the next generation of civic leaders. We work with a network of over 2,000 young people who have participated in our leadership programs. They are leading local initiatives that matter to them, from bringing drinkable water to their communities to advocating for human rights but they are also increasingly making up the ranks of leadership in public and private organizations. These efforts are allowing them to exercise their political muscle and see results.

As a result of USAID efforts, citizens are also holding municipal governments accountable, exercising democratic principles at a local level. Citizens have submitted nearly 200 proposals to extend services for youth, women, and the disabled in nine municipalities and nearly half of these proposals, worth over $1.6 million, have been incorporated in municipal budgets.

We are also strengthening independent media, as they face restrictive regulations and dwindling resources as advertisers pay a political cost for their support. USAID works with over 20 organizations in press, radio, and television to strengthen their operations and help them be more effective.

While democracy and governance remain USAID's priorities in Nicaragua, we also support citizen security and education in the autonomous Caribbean coast, where the worst poverty indicators exist. USAID education programs help improve early grade reading, which is an important determinant in keeping kids in school. Our vocational programs with the private sector are helping youth become employable with skills in carpentry, plumbing, car repairs, and ultimately become productive members of their society. The autonomous Caribbean region is home to the most isolated and vulnerable populations in Nicaragua and helping these populations prosper is also crucial to a thriving and healthy democracy.

USAID will continue to evaluate and adjust our programs in Nicaragua so that they remain effective and, looking forward, will continue to elevate Nicaragua's most prominent civil society organizations and connect them with organizations around the globe who are facing similar challenges. It is imperative that the U.S. Government continue to engage and stand by the people of Nicaragua. We are a lifeline that helps them advocate for their rights and freedoms in an increasingly challenging environment.

We share a commitment to democratic governance with our regional neighbors. As stated in the Inter-American Democratic Charter, the peoples of the Americas have a right to democracy and their governments have an obligation to promote and defend it.

I want to thank this committee again for your leadership and support and I look forward to your continued counsel and welcome your questions.

[The prepared statement of Ms. Escobari follows:]

Testimony of Marcela X. Escobari
Assistant Administrator for Latin America and the Caribbean
United States Agency for International Development (USAID)
Before the House Foreign Affairs Committee
Subcommittee for the Western Hemisphere
Thursday, September 15, 2016, 10:00 AM

Chairman Duncan, Ranking Member Sires, and members of the Subcommittee, thank you for the invitation to testify today. I am grateful for the Committee's support for the United States Agency for International Development's work in Latin America and the Caribbean, and am pleased to have this opportunity to testify before you today on our programming in Nicaragua.

Development Context
Under the *U.S. Strategy for Engagement in Central America* (the Strategy), USAID is working in Nicaragua to address the country's most urgent needs, including support for civil society, improved citizen security, and enhanced opportunity for youth, who make up 50 percent of the population. Our programs align with the priorities of the Strategy and are consistent with the Agency's mission of ending extreme poverty and promoting resilient, democratic societies while enhancing our prosperity and security. As the Government of Nicaragua increasingly consolidates its power through undemocratic means, this is a critical time to engage the people of Nicaragua in confronting the significant challenges they face.

The United States Government remains deeply concerned by the Nicaraguan Government's actions to close democratic space. According to the State Department's 2015 Human Rights report, independent media is increasingly muzzled and Nicaraguan citizens are regularly harassed for exercising their legal rights to free speech.[1] Since 2008, much of the international community has viewed national and local elections as flawed,[2] and the Nicaraguan government continues to demonstrate a troubling pattern of overreach. In January 2014, the Nicaraguan government instituted constitutional reforms to consolidate power in the executive branch, and in recent months, the Nicaraguan Supreme Court has taken even more dramatic steps to close democratic space and restrict electoral competition in advance of November 6, 2016 elections.

Nicaragua is the second poorest nation in the Western Hemisphere, with an estimated 30 percent of the population living below the poverty line.[3] Criminal activities and violence, particularly related to narco-trafficking, are on the rise along the country's Caribbean Coast. Between 2006 and 2012, the yearly homicide rate in the Southern Autonomous Caribbean Coast Region (RACCS) increased from 30 to 38 per 100,000 inhabitants (a 27 percent increase in six years), which put this region on par with Guatemala's homicide rate.[4]

---

[1] U.S. Department of State Human Rights Report 2015

[2] USAID/Nicaragua Country Development Cooperation Strategy FY 2013-FY 2017

[3] CIA World Fact Book 2015

[4] Rodriguez, Mariana; Donoso, Juan Carlos. March 2016. Final Baseline Report on Citizen Security in the Northern Autonomous Caribbean Coast in Nicaragua and Targeted Municipalities of the Northern and Southern Borders.

Despite reported gains in access to basic services, Nicaragua remains one of the most economically unequal countries in the world, ranked 132 of 187 by the World Bank.[5] In the Southern Autonomous Caribbean Coast Region, one of two areas where USAID targets its citizen security and education programming, 45 percent of school-age boys and 40 percent of girls are not in school.[6]

Democracy and Governance

USAID remains committed to supporting the Nicaraguan people, including civil society, as they demand a more open, transparent, and accountable government. Our democracy and governance programs, which account for 65 percent of our FY 2016 bilateral assistance to the country, seek to build an engaged citizenry that can address these challenges.

USAID's governance assistance helps civil society organizations advocate for citizen needs; promote democratic processes nationwide, such as the freedom of association; promote public policy dialogues; and demand accountability of public resources. Our programs also strengthen cohesion among civil society organizations to further enhance the effectiveness of their efforts.

Fifty percent of Nicaraguans are under the age of 25.[7] USAID's programs engage and empower the next generation to participate in democratic processes. We teach young people the rights and responsibilities of a democratic society, including the crucial need for meaningful political party presence and participation at the national and local levels. USAID has also developed specialized courses and leadership training for a core group of young political and civic leaders.

Alongside these efforts, USAID supports media programs that increase citizen advocacy for independent media, the right to freedom of expression, and access to public information. Our programs mentor young journalists, disseminate best practices for an independent media, and support media partners and civil society to better advocate for freedom of information.

Our efforts are making a difference. Of the more than 2,200 young leaders who have participated in youth leadership programs over the past five years, more than 300 have been promoted or appointed to key leadership positions in public and private organizations. Nearly 1,400 civic leaders representing 28 civil society organizations have received training on accessing public information, the municipal government budget process, and conducting social audits.

As a result of USAID's efforts, citizens are holding municipal governments accountable, exercising democratic practices at a local level. Nearly 200 proposals from citizens to extend services to youth, women, and the disabled have been submitted in nine municipalities. Nearly half of these proposals have been incorporated into municipal budgets, representing $1.6 million.

Independent media outlets face increasingly restrictive regulations, as well as dwindling resources from private sector advertisers who pay a political cost for their support. With USAID support, the Nicaraguan Chamber of Radio Stations is standardizing its advertising rates and

---

[5] World Bank 2013

[6] USAID 2012 Nicaragua Gender Analysis

[7] United Nations, Department of Economic and Social Affairs, Population Division. World Population Prospects: The 2015 Revision.

negotiating as a sector. This action is the first of its kind in the history of the Nicaraguan radio sector and represents a significant advance toward leveraging fair operating conditions.

Citizen Security and Opportunities for Youth
While democracy and governance programming remains USAID's primary focus in Nicaragua, we are also supporting two crucial and interdependent activities that underpin a thriving, healthy democracy: citizen security and education. Although Nicaragua's crime rates are lower than those of its regional neighbors, violent crime, narco-trafficking, trafficking in persons, and transnational organized crime are growing, particularly in the autonomous Caribbean Coast regions where we target our citizen security and education programs. These challenges have an especially negative impact on Nicaraguan youth, who have limited opportunities for licit employment, high dropout rates, low literacy rates, and are at risk for drug use and gang recruitment. The decline of Nicaragua's security is of domestic and regional concern and of strategic importance to the United States.

USAID's education programs help improve early grade reading and teacher training, and encourage youth to stay in school, with the aim of becoming productive and engaged citizens in their communities. We leverage private sector investment in vocational training for at-risk youth in needed disciplines such as carpentry, plumbing, and automobile repair. These programs include hard and soft skills-building to help youth become employable and more self-sufficient, which in turn frees them from the political pressure that takes place if they turn to politicized government social programs for support.

USAID's programs also focus on civic education throughout primary, secondary, and technical vocational training, and intentionally incorporate critical thinking skills and civic participation and engagement. These programs are taught outside of the classroom with parents and community members as they prioritize and design community action plans to improve elements of community security and education.

Regional Approach
USAID's regional programming supplements our bilateral assistance to Nicaragua to advance and promote human rights. We recently awarded a five-year $24.9 million regional program to strengthen national human rights organizations in Central America, including in Nicaragua.

USAID is also supporting investigative journalists in Latin America by promoting safe online collaboration, and empowering journalists with the tools and skills they need for research and investigation. USAID also supports a regional clearinghouse for investigative journalism, linking national investigative journalism centers into a powerful regional voice for journalists.

Oversight
USAID takes its responsibility to the United States taxpayer seriously, and we are committed to accountability, transparency, and oversight of our programs. Our Nicaragua Mission is guided by a five-year strategic plan and has developed a robust Monitoring, Evaluation, and Learning Plan. Monitoring and evaluation informs new program designs and where we need to make changes to existing programming.

USAID currently funds six democracy and governance activities in Nicaragua, the majority of which are operated by highly qualified U.S. organizations; the others are managed by leading local civil society organizations. In a country where there is an ever-present risk of government interference, we have partnered with organizations that combine the broad expertise of international democracy and governance organizations with local organizations with established presence and support base, making them harder to uproot. This blend of local and international expertise allows us to ensure that the gains that local civil society makes can be sustained.

As conditions deteriorate and power is consolidated in the Nicaraguan executive branch, the Agency will look at ways to adapt our programming to this new reality. We are considering new ways to support traditional civil society organizations to improve their efficacy in an increasingly hostile environment.

Conclusion
The U.S. Government supports full participation by the people of Nicaragua in their government. We believe that elections should be free, fair, and transparent, and that every vote should count. We echo the values enshrined in the Inter-American Democratic Charter: "The peoples of the Americas have a right to democracy and their governments have an obligation to promote and defend it. Democracy is essential for the social, political, and economic development of the peoples of the Americas."[8]

It is imperative that the U.S. Government continue to engage and stand by the people of Nicaragua, including youth and civil society, offering them a lifeline that helps them continue to advocate for their rights and freedom in an increasingly challenging time.

I would like to thank Members of Congress, and members of this Subcommittee in particular, for your continued leadership, interest in and support for our work. We look forward to collaborating with you to address long-standing challenges and new opportunities for reform. Thank you for your time; I welcome your questions.

---

[8] Organization of American States, Inter-American Democratic Charter, 2001

Mr. DUNCAN. I thank both the witnesses and will step out of the norm here and recognize the ranking member first for 5 minutes.

Mr. SIRES. I want to thank the chairman for his consideration. You know it is always bewildering to me how the second poorest country in the Western Hemisphere, basically, is buying tanks, is buying planes, is buying all sorts of arms and yet, the need of the people seems to be ignored.

So, I am just wondering if this is the typical intimidation factor that leaders that abolished democracy or tried to circumvent democracy usually use. Or why do you think he needs so much artillery, Warren—or I am sorry—Mr. Gonzalez? Like my buddy.

Mr. GONZALEZ. Thank you, Congressman. So, you are exactly right, actually, Nicaragua is the second poorest country in the Western Hemisphere. What we have seen, however, is that even though he won and actually observed the 2006 election when Ortega came back to power. He won with just roughly 38 percent of the vote.

Today, he enjoys 60 percent or so level of popularity and a lot of that has been as a result of a lot of the social investments that he has made in the country. There have been reductions in poverty, even though the level of poverty remains above 39 percent but a lot of it is a result of Venezuela's largess. And in our view, it is not sustainable, particularly, in the absence of strong institutions.

Every country has the right to buy military equipment. And is it something that they are using as a tool of intimidation? What is clear to us is that the approach that Ortega has actually been using since 2006 have been overt efforts to consolidate one-party control, something he has been working on since he returned, remove even independent allies within Sandinista, repress civil society, independent media, and the opposition, control the private sector and advance an active propaganda for the Sandinista party.

But to answer your questions, sir, there is this old Latin American saying, which is for our friends, anything and for our enemies, the law. So, they are using a way to actually technically using legal systems to undermine the opposition in a way that is bad for the country's democracy and for the thriving of civil society.

Mr. SIRES. Thank you. Marcela?

Ms. ESCOBARI. So, I would just agree with your comment that we agree that the Nicaraguan Government should be focusing more on its poor, particularly the Caribbean Coast, which is an isolated area with the most vulnerable populations and we have seen violence and poverty increase in those areas.

Mr. SIRES. Thank you. And through this process, Daniel Ortega and his family have become very wealthy in the last few terms, I understand that one of the richest in Nicaragua. Is that accurate?

Mr. GONZALEZ. Well, I know that the wealthiest 10 percent receive roughly 39 percent of all income and that right now the bottom 30 percent receive roughly 8.3 percent. So, there is a huge level of inequality that endures in Nicaragua.

Mr. SIRES. Yes, but I am talking about the President and his family.

Mr. GONZALEZ. I could get you information. I don't have the details on his personal wealth.

Mr. SIRES. But he is doing much better than he has done before, right?

Mr. GONZALEZ. I imagine, yes.

Mr. SIRES. You are being a good politician here.

Thank you, Mr. Chairman.

Mr. DUNCAN. I thank the ranking member.

I am now going to go ahead and recognize Mr. Yoho for 5 minutes.

Mr. YOHO. Thank you, Mr. Chairman. I appreciate the meeting here.

And I want to spin off of my colleague, Mr. Sires, about here we are the second poorest country in the Western Hemisphere, yet, they are buying tanks and planes from Russia. And we engage in the IMET Initiative, the International Military and Education Training. What are we benefitting out of this? Are we showing them our techniques and our skills and all that? And they are using Russian forces. Is that benefitting us and who are they preparing for an invasion from? Or is it like Ms. Ros-Lehtinen said, to keep oppression on the people?

Mr. GONZALEZ. Congressman, thank you for your question.

The IMET support that we provide to Nicaragua, I have got to say that they are not allowing members of the Nicaraguan military to actually come up here. And I think it is, my interpretation is because what we actually do through IMET training is create a professional military. We promote the respect for human rights. We find synergies between U.S. and foreign militaries and it has been an effective took for us to cooperate with foreign militaries around the world.

Mr. YOHO. Let me interrupt you there. You said we respect their rights for human rights or their initiative on that.

Mr. GONZALEZ. Well, the types of classes that we teach through IMET where we will bring people up here is a series of classes that include human rights, better interoperability with U.S. military, those types of trainings. They have not actually allowed Nicaraguan military to come up for the training.

Mr. YOHO. All right, I want to drop back and come back to that because how do you hold a dictatorship like Ortega accountable when we know they are doing what they are doing? They are dealing in human trafficking. They said there is not a lot of narco trafficking but how do we know that is true? We know the heroin is coming across the Mexican border. Where does the heroin come from?

Mr. GONZALEZ. Well, we have actually concrete results in cooperating with them on counter-narcotics.

Mr. YOHO. Well, again, where is the heroin coming from? We know it is coming across the Mexican border into America. Where does it come from in South America?

Mr. GONZALEZ. Well, the source countries include Colombia, I would say, primarily but——

Mr. YOHO. Okay, so how does it get from there to Mexico, to the United States, if it is not coming through Nicaragua? Are they going around that? Are they going through that and we don't know about it and we are facilitating with our military intelligence, giving them foreign aid and teaching them our counter narcotics methods?

Is that helping us or is it helping them circumvent our counter narcotics interdiction?

Mr. GONZALEZ. It actually helps us because it instills, it aligns values, in a way, actually, of how you manage responsible and a political military.

In terms of the flow of drugs, cocaine and heroin that come up to the United States, they go by land and by air. Mostly, they will skip over Nicaragua, even though they are, right now I think in 2015 we seized over 4.3 metric tons of cocaine but a lot of them are overshooting and going to other countries or going, obviously, still through land but in lower numbers because Nicaragua has actually been very active on the counter-narcotics front.

Mr. YOHO. All right and then let me ask you this, Ms. Escobari, if you would answer. How are we going to respond if the elections are run as a mockery to democracy in their country with a constitution that says he can't run another term, his wife can't be there? How are we going to respond?

And I would also like to know about the hypocrisy of what happened in Honduras when their President ran for the third term and the people of that country stood by their constitution and pulled him out but, yet our administration, along with Ms. Clinton, said that we can't do that; we have to stand by that President of that nation. But yet, the opposite is happening here and where is the outcry from the administration?

So, what are we going to do, the first question is, after this election and it is a mockery? What is this administration's response going to be?

Ms. ESCOBARI. Well, thank you, Congressman for your question.

And it is true, we are also very troubled about the lack of electoral observers in this election. Through USAID, we are working to continue to push for accountability. We are even running up to the election. We are working with youth organizations that are able to monitor fraudulent election practices and misuse of funds. During the election, we are also going to have volunteers who are going to try to be in polling stations and report on——

Mr. YOHO. How effective is that? I mean you have got youth monitoring that but you have got a country that has tanks and all that other stuff. How realistic is that?

Ms. ESCOBARI. No, absolutely, this is not the ideal situation. And we very much regret the setbacks in a fair electoral procedure.

And we are mentioning here the things that we are trying to do just not to stay quiet and to continue to try to push for accountability and at least make sure that there are observers and they are able to share with the Nicaraguans and outside, if things continue to proceed as they——

Mr. YOHO. I am out of time and I will yield back. If there is another round, we will come back to that. Thank you.

Mr. DUNCAN. Thank you, Chairman.

Now, we will go to Mr. Castro.

Mr. CASTRO. Thank you, Chair.

Let me ask you all about Nicaragua's involvement with Russia and China. What is the extent of those two nations' involvement with Nicaragua?

Mr. GONZALEZ. Thank you, Congressman. So, separate from Russia and China, whenever a third country is involved in Latin America or Central America and promoting a hemisphere that Vice President Biden calls secure middle class and democratic and is abiding by international rules, it is not a zero sum game. We say welcome. You can't take those roads with you when you build them.

Specifically to your question, sir, Russia has seen itself specifically isolated over the past several years, as they face international outcry over its incursions in other parts of the world. And so they have tried to increase their engagement. If you seize the countries that they have an opening with, like Nicaragua, are few and far between. The engagement tends to be transactional. And it is something we are watching very closely but we see it as limited and to arms sales and resulting spare parts and training as a part of the main part of the relationship.

Mr. CASTRO. Is there a foreign aid component from either of those countries over Nicaragua that you all know of?

Mr. GONZALEZ. Well, with regard to Russia, they will provide credits. As you know, they sold the tanks to Nicaragua. But beyond that, it has been mostly just a transactional arms trading exercise.

It is something that we are watching very closely and it is something that we would welcome an opportunity to brief you in a classified setting. I know we have discussed this with the chairman in a classified setting before and welcome that opportunity.

Mr. CASTRO. Sure. Did you have something? Okay.

And can you describe the status of our security cooperation under CARSI and how that is coming along?

Mr. GONZALEZ. Yes, so Congressman, our assistance that focuses on Central America is one that does not go directly to the government. We providing training, equipment and so on and so forth. Overall, we are going to provide $13 million in 2016 funds and the impact is one where we have actually worked with the Nicaraguan Navy, which even though it has really limited assets, conducts regular patrols and interdiction operations in their internal waters in the Pacific and in the Caribbean Coast. We have donated equipment. They are actually using donated Nor-Tech Boston Whalers and refurbished boats under Section 1033 authority, which is the DoD money but it something that has synergies with the Central American Regional Security Initiative.

And the support, again, is the work that we do is there will be training and we will provide equipment that is specifically focused toward the counter-narcotics operation. The results have been, as I mentioned earlier, 4.3 metric tons in seized assets last year. So far, they have arrested over 135 people, seized $2.8 million and 55 go-fast boats and other means of transport. And so we are having a lot of results in that area of cooperation.

Mr. CASTRO. And also, Nicaragua is party to CAFTA, right?

Mr. GONZALEZ. That is correct.

Mr. CASTRO. What effect has that had on the country?

Mr. GONZALEZ. Well, it has actually been significant. Actually, our trade, two-way trade has doubled in the past decade. We have a $5 billion trade relationship and our exports have increased 25 percent in 2015 or up 18 percent as far as July of this year.

But Congressman, to the point on the democracies, we could do so much more to cooperate with Nicaragua in the way that we do with other parts of Central America. But because of the limiting of democratic freedoms, we have a very limited scope in which we work with the government.

Mr. CASTRO. Okay, thank you.

Mr. DUNCAN. We will take just a second.

[Recess.]

Mr. DUNCAN. For the record, Chairwoman Ros-Lehtinen was a great chairwoman of the Foreign Affairs Committee. She was very fair to me when I was a freshman member. So, I would do anything for her.

I let her catch her breath and the Chair recognizes——

Ms. ROS-LEHTINEN. Thank you, Mr. Chairman. Thank you. And I have been listening to the testimony and the questions from the side room. So, I appreciate your testimony and the questions from the members.

Secretary Gonzalez, I would first like to thank you for working closely with our committee and staff. My staff has briefed me on how helpful you have been with providing information and briefings regarding Nicaragua. So, I want to say gracias, that we appreciate your work on this issue. And as you have just witnessed, before the hearing, we had the markup. We passed the Nicaragua legislation in a bipartisan manner.

Do you think that this legislation helps advance U.S. efforts to hold the Ortega regime accountable for its violations against human rights and electoral manipulation?

Mr. GONZALEZ. Madam Chair, thank you for your words. First of all, I think the most important lesson Vice President Joe Biden taught me was taking very seriously the advice and consent role of the U.S. Congress. So, it has been a pleasure to work with you and your staff.

So, while we cannot comment on pending legislation, I will say, Madam Chair, that we share the principles behind it and, frankly, the work that this committee and that you personally doing to spotlight the challenges in Nicaragua. So, we share the principles but I cannot comment on the specifics.

Ms. ROS-LEHTINEN. Absolutely. I understand.

Also, press reports have indicated that the Ortega regime will now exercise control over diplomatic pouches. This is very troubling. Is this accurate? And if so, how will this impact the work of our U.S. Embassy officials and its staff?

Mr. GONZALEZ. Madam Chair, my understanding is that they are going to—they have announced that they will begin using an x-ray of packages, which is something that they can do under international law but it is something we are watching very closely because any step beyond that to maybe move to open it would be something that would be in violation of their international obligations and would be troubling to us in the course of——

Ms. ROS-LEHTINEN. Well, thank you for that.

And Administrator Escobari, thank you so much. It was a pleasure meeting with you just yesterday.

Congress brought back USAID back into Cuba, as we fast tracked your congressional notification last year, yet it took over 6 months to get the program dollars out the door. In Venezuela, USAID decided to cut the democratic program dollars last year to $3.2 million. While this was quickly corrected after congressional intervention, I worry about the signal that this sends about USAID's commitment to promoting democracy efforts. We can't let the fear of possibly being expelled from the country from scaring USAID from cooperating in closed societies. And in Nicaragua, USAID has failed to improve the democracy programs in Nicaragua for years. And in 2012, I sent a letter to USAID stating that funds to Nicaragua have not been spent wisely and prohibited funds from being used in the Ortega-controlled municipalities or from being used to work with the Ortega regime. Yet, just months ago, committee staff traveled to Nicaragua and USAID officials requested flexibility in order to work with officials from the Ortega regime and that is just simply unacceptable.

How can we work together in order to improve the democracy programs in Nicaragua? I know that is your goal. That is our goal as well. How can we help Nicaraguan civil society who are being oppressed on a daily basis? And related to that, if you can share with us some success, in terms of human rights and democracy, the program that you have from USAID programs. Is the country more democratic and with stronger civil society and empowered human rights organizations now? Thank you.

Ms. ESCOBARI. Thank you very much Madam Chairman.

At USAID, we totally share your concerns and your focus on democratic programming. And it actually makes up the priority of our bilateral funding to Nicaragua. If you ask me, I think the last years have witnessed more democracy and governance setbacks than gains and it has become a more challenging environment to work in.

That said, we continue to support over 60 civil society organizations, local organizations, both through international partners and through directly with many of them and we are trying to strengthen them. For many of them, we are their only lifeline, as many other donors have left.

We have also started working with younger people and organizations that advocate for democratic principles at a local level. And we are also working with independent media, which we believe is a very important force that needs to remain open and is facing increasing challenges in this environment.

Ms. ROS-LEHTINEN. Thank you very much, Mr. Chairman. Thank you for allowing me to speak and for the markup earlier today. Thank you, sir.

Mr. DUNCAN. You are welcome. Anytime.

I now recognize myself for 5 minutes. And I would like to start with the expulsion of three U.S. citizens in Nicaragua, Mr. Gonzalez.

On June 13th, three U.S. citizens traveling on openly cleared U.S. official government business were kicked out of Nicaragua. Such actions suggest flagrant disrespect by the Ortega Government for commonly accepted principles of government-to-government relations.

Given the erosion of democracy in Nicaragua, the clear contempt that Nicaragua has displayed in its government-to-government relationship with the U.S., is it appropriate to continue to reward Nicaragua with a virtually unrestricted access to U.S. markets that the nation receives under CAFTA?

Mr. GONZALEZ. Mr. Chairman, thank you for that question.

While it is the right of every nation to control its borders and who enters and, obviously, official interaction, we agree. We coincide entirely with you that the expulsion was unwarranted and inconsistent with a constructive and positive bilateral relationship.

Immediately after, the two officials who were actually there to facilitate trade on textiles, I, personally, spoke with Ambassador Campbell and made clear the potential ramifications of going down this road. We communicated a diplomatic note and, since then, actually, clarified the travel procedures with the Nicaraguan Government.

Since then, we have not had problems. And we know that there have been religious organizations and faith-based organizations that have been interested in doing work, we have had journalists and others.

Since the new travel procedures have been established, we have been able to go forward without incident but we have made it clear that we will have to reconsider how we respond if this is something that continues.

Mr. DUNCAN. Given the fact that Nicaragua is one of the poorest countries in Central America, who do you think benefits the most from a free trade agreement with the United States, the United States or Nicaragua?

You don't need to answer that. I think Nicaragua does. You are a diplomat. I am a politician.

Nicaragua benefits from that access to the United States but we continue to see things like this happen and the United States goes right back in and continues to cozy up to these countries, when the countries have sort of thumbed their nose at the U.S. This has happened in Venezuela in the past. It is now happening here. And it is definitely happening in Cuba.

So, let me ask you this. I have got concerns with U.S. Ambassador Dogu's actions. So, on June 8th, the Nicaraguan Supreme Court stripped the opposition Independent Liberal Party from its recognized leader and Ortega's 2006 Presidential challenger, Eduardo Montealegre—I can't pronounce that. My Spanglish isn't that good. So, it put in the party under control of a government-allied leader.

On June 17th, the Supreme Court invalidated the leadership of the Citizen Action Party, the only remaining party with a legal standing to present a Presidential candidate. This also disqualified the Presidential candidate Luis Callejas and Ortega's main challenge for the November 6th election.

So, let's get rid of all of our political opponents, using the Supreme Court to do that. But then recently, U.S. Ambassador Laura Dogu paid a visit to Nicaragua's Supreme Court. She shouldn't have dignified them by visiting them. So, why did that visit take place?

Mr. GONZALEZ. Mr. Chairman, first on the trade point, I just want to say that it is in our interest to actually engage with the Nicaraguan people and trade. While it does benefit the economic elites, it also benefits the people.

But we are looking at, as the elections progress and coincide with everything that you have said on the treatment of political opposition, we are looking at all of our tools at our disposal, understanding that there is no silver bullet and that the Nicaraguans have to be the ones that decide the future of their country.

The Ambassador Dogu, who has been very active on the ground, we coincided that diplomatic engagement is not a reward. It is an opportunity to actually make very clear what our concerns are. And whenever she meets with the Supreme Court and she meets just as much with members of the opposition, civil society and youth, and the government, makes very clear what our concerns are and where U.S. policy is headed. And so we feel like she has been very effective in that regard.

Now, just very briefly on the political situation. I don't need to tell this committee that the political process involves constant compromise. But in the United States, we are not perfect. Our democracy is always improving. But we speak out on these sorts of issues not because we are perfect but because we think the ideal of not persecuting people if they disagree with you is the right ideal, number one. And we do not have, as Americans, confidence in a system where one person or one family is making all of the decisions.

And we believe that in a democracy, if we believe in democracy, it means everybody has to have a chance to speak out and actually offer their views. And that is what being undermined in Nicaragua and I think, in the long-run, will not be good for the country.

Mr. DUNCAN. Let me just say this. I think if a country is a recipient of the money from the U.S. taxpayers for economic assistance and USAID and all of this, and we are trying to court or support democracy and free elections, and individual liberties, humanitarian rights, and those sort of things, these countries ought to, personally ought to be a little more friendly to the United States. And kicking out diplomats, and I don't know all of the details of that, but I disagree from what I know.

So, let me just ask one other question and then I will move on. The United States supports OAS. OAS supports democratic principles throughout the region. And you are not representing the OAS but I would ask your opinion on why the OAS hasn't been any stronger in its stance over what has gone on in Nicaragua with regard to the elections because the elections are the core of democracy.

So, why would you think the OAS hasn't been stronger in this instance? And we have seen the OAS really take not stringent enough positions against Venezuela. So, why wouldn't the OAS be stronger here?

Mr. GONZALEZ. Mr. Chairman, on your first point, we coincide entirely. One of the strategies that the Ortega administration has taken is to actually essentially control the private sector, under the presumption that as long as they have good counter-narcotics cooperation with the United States and a good relationship with the private sector, they pay their international debts, that we will turn a blind eye to the undermining of democracy.

This will have, I think—we are approaching a situation where in November they will be free, in the sense that people will be allowed to vote in the election. But they will not be fair and it is something that over time will undermine, I think, how the institutions work and it will have implications for the private sector. And it is something that in Nicaragua but around the hemisphere and around the world, Secretary Kerry, our Acting Assistant Secretary Mari Carmen Aponte have made anti-corruption efforts a priority.

And we have taken actions even with our allies in places like Honduras. You have seen our work in Guatemala and it is something that we are looking at everything we have in our diplomatic toolbox to see how we can actually tackle these sorts of issues of corruption, violations of human rights, et cetera. I look forward to working with you and your committee on developing those tools most effectively.

On the OAS briefly, sir, we have done everything possible to try to get the Government to agree to invite an electoral observation machine. I will note that the OAS is observing the U.S. election. So, it is not that we are saying do what we say and not do what we do, we are actually walking the walk in this case.

And the OAS is actually looking very closely at the situation in Nicaragua. I understand they are working on a report that they will release. And the reality is that currently the time is closing for there to be an international observation mission and that the conditions maybe don't exist for there to be a fair election, as I mentioned.

Mr. DUNCAN. I didn't mean to put you in a predicament there talking about the OAS but when I read of the history of the OAS, I am pro-OAS. I know what it was founded for. I know what it is supposed to be doing with regard to democratic principles in the region but I think we are approaching at point, to use your term, we are approaching a point where the OAS is becoming less effective because they continue to kind of deviate or water down their traditional stances in those regards, with regard to Nicaragua, in this case, Venezuela.

So, I would say that if the OAS was sitting here. I think they need to go back, reread their founding documents, reread their charter and come to a meeting of the minds on what they exist for because this is a prime example, where they need to—it shows a little bit more outrage with regard to what the Supreme Court in Nicaragua has done and taking it even one step further, what Maduro is doing in Venezuela with not allowing a recall when the Constitution of Venezuela calls for that. And when you believe in those democratic constitutional principles, you have got to adhere to that and OAS says we are going to support the democratic principles. So, where is the outrage for those founding principles?

So, I am going to stop there. And I will now go to Mr. Castro, if he has got another round of questions.

Mr. CASTRO. Thank you, Chairman.

I have a question on Nicaragua and energy. Nicaragua does not produce oil and has long been dependent on imported fuel oil to generate electricity. My understanding is that Nicaragua has recently invested heavily in renewable energy, wind, solar, and geothermal, in particular. So, my question is, has the U.S. played a supporting role in this transformation and can Nicaragua's renewable energy transformation be replicated across the hemisphere.

Mr. GONZALEZ. Thank you, Mr. Congressman, for that very important question.

One of the initiatives that when I was with Vice President Biden that we launched with our State Department Special Envoy for Energy Issues, Amos Hochstein, was the Caribbean Energy Security Initiative in June 2014 but then it is something that we also rolled out in Central America.

And on the premise that the region's dependence on expensive imported fuel provides headwinds to development and efforts to actually reduce poverty. And what we have been doing in Nicaragua has actually been we have been taking a regional approach.

The countries have what is called the SIEPAC line, which allows them to coordinate in the transmission of electricity and it is something that is not being taken full advantage of. And it is something we are trying to provide technical assistance through kind of the regional energy market to help them actually take full advantage and get to the point where they can expand the capacity but also, because cooperation on energy issues between states is incredibly complicated, try to find a way to ensure that renewable energy is something that is integrated into the grid and not just traditional fossil fuels.

Costa Rica and Nicaragua have actually taken very active steps on renewables. Honduras is making investments. And I think the positive consequences or results of our engagement have been that we are trying to streamline the way they do regulation, the way they take advantage of the line, and how they actually start expanding the use of renewables.

Mr. CASTRO. Thank you. And then a question about the Chinese canal that is being built. How likely is it that Inter-Oceanic Canal underwritten by Chinese billionaire Wang Jing will actually be completed? And what implications does construction of the canal have for China-Nicaragua relations and Chinese involvement in the country?

Mr. GONZALEZ. Congressman, perhaps this will sound undiplomatic but I am skeptical. We have not seen a single shovel being used in the building of the Nicaragua Canal. And so the position we will take is we will believe it when we see it.

But it is something that we are watching, I think, very closely. The expansion of the Panama Canal is something that benefits U.S. ports in a significant way, because it allows us to reduce our shipping costs. And so, it is something that we are watching.

With regard to China's involvement, whether it is in Nicaragua or in the Caribbean, where they have also been very present, the message we have always conveyed to them is that there are international standards that all of us have to uphold and that insofar as they are upholding those and they are promoting secure, prosperous, and democratic region, we are welcoming their engagement. But we maintain a yearly active dialogue with the Chinese on Latin America and how best to actually maximize their cooperation in a productive way.

Mr. CASTRO. Thank you. I yield back.

Mr. DUNCAN. Great questions, Mr. Castro.

I will go to Mr. Yoho for 5 minutes or as much time as he needs.

Mr. YOHO. Thank you, Mr. Chairman. I appreciate it.

And I kind of want to spin off a couple of things here but I want to read a statement here that Mr. Ortega said in Cuba. The current President Daniel Ortega gave a speech in Havana, Cuba, affirming Sandinista policies and ideology in joining the Non-Aligned Movement and in excoriating the imperialism of the U.S. That was a statement he made. Do you feel he has wavered from that or varied from that in his stance toward the U.S.?

Mr. GONZALEZ. I can't pretend to know what is in the mind of President Daniel Ortega but I know that often, be it Nicaragua or be it Venezuela, often the moniker of U.S. imperialism is a foil to distract from problems inside the country but also, I think, as a way to I think maybe brandish a sort of socialist—or not socialist—a sort of way of governing and try to push out any sort of——

Mr. YOHO. I think we can tell where he stands with actions, when you see what they do. You know you are looking at the amount of corruption there and you look at the wealth. He is one of the wealthiest people in the country that is the second poorest country in the Western Hemisphere. And then you look at the loan that Venezuela gave them back a few years back, I think it was $457 million with no third-party oversight, it is a very convenient situation.

And then they are buying Russian military equipment. They are putting up Russian military radar systems. And I am not feeling the love here. And I, along with the chairman, you know he was talking about the trade, the free trade agreement that we have with them, I don't see the benefit we do. I see we do export but I think they are benefitting a whole lot more. And the benefit to them is they have a lot of money coming into their country that is promoting a rogue—a dictatorship, I will say. And with the administrator's misstep of sending our Ambassador Dogu down there and allowing them to basically give credit to their Supreme Court for ruling out any competing parties in the political process, I just think that is a very poor judgment and misstep on this administration.

We have all these conditions on trade. We have all these conditions on human rights. We have all these conditions on free and open elections and he has already said there is not going to be free and open elections because there is not going to be any monitors but yet, we are relying on the students to tell us how fair they are.

How intimidated are those students going to be and how well are they going to speak up? And at what point does administration say, you know what, if you are going to play by the rules, we are done and pull out of the trade agreement?

Do we have the backbone to do that? Does this administration have it or any administration? When is America's word going to stand for what we say?

Mr. GONZALEZ. Congressman, I will say two things. And thank you for your comments. We coincide entirely on the democratic backsliding in Nicaragua.

Two things. First——

Mr. YOHO. Well, then we are not doing it with action.

Let me ask Ms. Escobari. Is that close? What is your opinion on that? At what point does America say if you are serious about being an ally of ours? Because we have weakened the OAS and it is because of the actions. If our action is not standing up to—our words aren't backed up by our actions.

Ms. ESCOBARI. Thank you, Congressman. For our case, the majority of our programming is trying to strengthen the few and usually harassed organizations that are trying to defend democratic institutions and citizens.

Mr. YOHO. How do you see them strengthening, if they are throwing people out that have diplomatic or regular passports and our administration is validating their Supreme Court?

Ms. ESCOBARI. No, you are absolutely right that there has not been progress. There has been backsliding but we believe that we should still be there to stand with those organizations to continue to maintain some openness and to have these organizations that can speak for the citizens as that closes.

Mr. YOHO. Yes, but if we are not willing to take something back for that government to lose, it is not going to get better. I mean history repeats itself. And until we are willing to stand up and make a strong stand, they are going to keep doing what they are doing and we are going to keep capitulating. And yes, we can say we are helping the people, which I think we should, but you have to hold that government accountable and you have to be willing to do that is what I see.

And I yield back and I appreciate the second round, Chairman.

Mr. DUNCAN. All right. This has been great. Do you have anything further?

I want to thank the panel. Nicaragua is not a country that, since I have been here 6 years, other than when Chairwoman Ros-Lehtinen was active in my first term, have we really delved into this. But what we are seeing, as brought out today, is just some things that we may not agree with going on with free and fair elections, and humanitarian rights, and strong military changes, and whatnot down there.

So, we are going to continue focusing on it and I want to thank the service of our witnesses to our great Nation. And it is not lost on us, the sacrifices you make as well. So, thank you so much.

I want to thank the committee for all of their participation, not only on the hearing but also on the markup.

And without anything further, we will stand adjourned.

[Whereupon, at 11:43 a.m., the subcommittee was adjourned.]

APPENDIX

MATERIAL SUBMITTED FOR THE RECORD

SUBCOMMITTEE HEARING NOTICE
COMMITTEE ON FOREIGN AFFAIRS
U.S. HOUSE OF REPRESENTATIVES
WASHINGTON, DC 20515-6128

Subcommittee on the Western Hemisphere
Jeff Duncan (R-SC), Chairman

TO: MEMBERS OF THE COMMITTEE ON FOREIGN AFFAIRS

You are respectfully requested to attend an OPEN markup and hearing of the Committee on Foreign Affairs, to be held in Room 2172 of the Rayburn House Office Building (and available live on the Committee website at http://www.ForeignAffairs.house.gov):

DATE: Thursday, September 15, 2016

TIME: 10:00 a.m.

SUBJECT: Nicaragua's Democratic Collapse

WITNESSES: Mr. Juan Gonzalez
Deputy Assistant Secretary
Bureau of Western Hemisphere Affairs
U.S. Department of State

The Honorable Marcela Escobari
Assistant Administrator
Bureau for Latin America and the Caribbean
U.S. Agency for International Development

By Direction of the Chairman

The Committee on Foreign Affairs seeks to make its facilities accessible to persons with disabilities. If you are in need of special accommodations, please call 202/225-5021 at least four business days in advance of the event, whenever practicable. Questions with regard to special accommodations in general (including availability of Committee materials in alternative formats and assistive listening devices) may be directed to the Committee.

COMMITTEE ON FOREIGN AFFAIRS

MINUTES OF SUBCOMMITTEE ON _____ *the Western Hemisphere* _____ HEARING

Day __*Thursday*__ Date _____*09/15/2016*_____ Room_____*2172*_____

Starting Time __*10:39 AM*__ Ending Time _*11:43 AM*_

Recesses __*n/a*__ (____to ____) (____to ____) (____to ____) (____to ____) (____to ____) (____to ____)

Presiding Member(s)

Chairman Jeff Duncan

Check all of the following that apply:

Open Session ☑   Electronically Recorded (taped) ☑
Executive (closed) Session ☐   Stenographic Record ☑
Televised ☑

TITLE OF HEARING:

Nicaragua's Democratic Collapse

SUBCOMMITTEE MEMBERS PRESENT:

Chairman Jeff Duncan, Ranking Member Albio Sires, Rep. Ileana Ros-Lehtinen, Rep. Matt Salmon, Rep. Ted Yoho, Rep. Dan Donovan, Rep. Joaquin Castro, Rep. Alan Grayson

NON-SUBCOMMITTEE MEMBERS PRESENT: *(Mark with an * if they are not members of full committee.)*

n/a

HEARING WITNESSES: Same as meeting notice attached? Yes ☑ No ☐
(If "no", please list below and include title, agency, department, or organization.)

STATEMENTS FOR THE RECORD: *(List any statements submitted for the record.)*

n/a

TIME SCHEDULED TO RECONVENE _____
or
TIME ADJOURNED ___*11:43 AM*___

Subcommittee Staff Associate

FINAL

BY ELECTRONIC SUBMISSION

Division of Dockets Management
Food and Drug Administration (HFA-305)
Department of Health and Human Services

To Whom It May Concern:

Cigar Rights of America serves as the sole voice of premium cigar consumers
in the United States of America on matters of legislative and regulatory concern,
with a membership that spans all 50 states. In addition, CRA members include
professional retail tobacconists and "Main Street America," and serve as an historic
and social component of the community fabric for those who enjoy premium cigars.
However, the cornerstone of CRA is that it is the largest preeminent coalition of
premium cigar manufacturers in the world, with representation of over 60 diverse
artisan producers of hand-made premium cigars. This coalition ranges from those
that conduct business on an international scale, to the single proprietorship
craftsman, who simply wants to produce great hand-made premium cigars. The
coalition also includes the entire spectrum of the supply chain, including
distributors, growers, mail-order houses, logistics, and associated supporting
enterprises. The manufacturer members of CRA are predominantly family owned
and entrepreneurial small businesses, built upon the skills that have often been
passed down from generation to generation.

A. Action Requested

The undersigned believes that premium cigars must be exempted from any
finalized Deeming regulation.[1]

B. Statement of Grounds

I. Economic Impact on Foreign Countries Will Be Profound

Under Executive Orders 12866 and 13563, FDA is required to take into account,
and to include in its economic analysis of the proposed Deeming rule, any trade and
international economic impacts that may result from the provisions. FDA has not

---

[1] *See* Deeming Tobacco Products To Be Subject to the Federal Food, Drug, and Cosmetic Act, as
Amended by the Family Smoking Prevention and Tobacco Control Act; Regulations on the Sale and
Distribution of Tobacco Products and Required Warning Statements for Tobacco Products, 79 Fed. Reg.
23142 (April 25, 2014).

done this, and the Agency ignores substantial costs for foreign growers and potentially extremely large job losses in foreign countries.

95% of handmade cigars are manufactured in foreign countries, primarily in Latin America. In Honduras, Nicaragua and the Dominican Republic alone, handmade cigars account for over 350,000 estimated jobs in the agricultural, craftsman, production, support services and distribution sectors. Premium cigar tobacco also create jobs in Cameroon and the Central African Republic – about 3,000 jobs in each country as well as Ecuador, Brazil, Columbia, Puerto Rico, Costa Rica, Peru, Panama, Indonesia, and Mexico. Each of these countries is certain to experience the adverse economic consequences of the FDA rule. While it is difficult to assign precise job-loss figures, FDA's own analysis claims that as many as 50% of cigar brands will be eliminated from commerce, a figure that CRA believes (and elsewhere demonstrates) is a lower bound estimate. Those figures imply huge losses of revenue in all affected countries and threaten 50%-80% of the 350,000 jobs throughout the Latin American premium cigar supply chain.

The governments of these countries have on several occasions communicated their concerns to their counterparts in the State Department and National Security Council and the former Ambassador to the United States from the Dominican Republic testified before the House Foreign Affairs Committee's Subcommittee on Western Hemisphere that the proposed regulations would have a dramatic impact on that nation's people. Nevertheless, FDA has failed to take into account the concerns as expressed by the Ambassador about the economic and political consequences for his country.

If FDA intends to finalize its proposed Deeming regulation, it must include analysis of the impacts on these countries in its Final Regulatory Impact Analysis, and it should use that information to conclude that premium cigars should not be included in the rule.

Dominican Republic, Honduras and Nicaragua

These three nations form the foundation of the Latin America premium cigar industry. With an estimated 300,000 – 350,000 jobs associated with the agricultural, production and distribution logistics of the industry, these jobs exist in most economically and politically sensitive region. On January 29, 2013, the Ambassadors to the United States from each of these three nations signed a joint letter to the State Department, U.S. Food & Drug Administration, and the National Security Council expressing serious concern as to what the regulation of the premium cigar industry would mean to the region.

The significance of the region was further noted when the Vice President announced a funding initiative for Central America ($1 billion) in which Honduras was specifically noted.

Ecuador

Ecuador has become a principle provider of premium cigar leaf, growing exponentially in popularity, specifically with American consumers. Any threat to production as a result of regulation, can adversely affect the agricultural contribution Ecuador makes to the premium cigar industry.

Mexico

Mexico has become a principle provider of premium cigar leaf, as well as wrapper and filler tobaccos, and has been growing exponentially in popularity, specifically with American consumers. Any threat to production as a result of regulation, can adversely affect the agricultural contribution Mexico makes to the premium cigar industry.

Mexico also has premium cigar manufacturing facilities that would be subject to any proposed regulatory program, making this issue a concern as it pertains to NAFTA implications.

Brazil

Brazil has become a principle provider of premium cigar leaf, growing exponentially in popularity, specifically with American consumers. Any threat to production as a result of regulation, can adversely affect the agricultural contribution Brazil makes to the premium cigar industry.

Indonesia

Indonesia has become a principle provider of premium cigar leaf, specifically for binders and fillers, growing in popularity, specifically with American consumers. Any threat to production as a result of regulation, can adversely affect the agricultural contribution Indonesia makes to the premium cigar industry.

Cameroon

Cameroon is a principle provider of premium cigar leaf, and specifically for prized cigar premium cigar wrapper that is vital to the Latin America – United States premium cigar market. Any threat to production as a result of regulation, can adversely affect the agricultural contribution Cameroon makes to the premium cigar industry.

II.   The Proposed Rule Is a Technical Barrier to Trade

As stated above, approximately 95% of handmade cigars sold in the United States are imported. The user fees that the FDA would impose on premium cigar manufacturers or importers erects a barrier to the importation of the roughly 260 million premium cigars that are currently imported each year, primarily from Latin America. Consequently, the user fee would place a burden on commerce between the United States and the Caribbean Basin countries, thereby violating the spirit of the Dominican Republic-Central America Free Trade Agreement ("DR- CAFTA").

A central theme that orbited the signing of DR-CAFTA was that to keep our economy growing and creating jobs, we need to open markets for American products overseas, as well as strengthening the regional economies within the hemisphere. We understood at the time that strengthening our regional economic ties is vital to America's economic and national security interests. Furthermore, we understood that by strengthening economic ties with nations in our hemisphere, we were advancing the stability that comes from such economic relationships. The purpose of DR-CAFTA was to facilitate trade between the United States and its Latin and Caribbean neighbors, noting that the imposition of a user fee on imported cigars undermines this goal.

Similarly, there are premium cigars imported from Mexico. For the same reason, FDA's proposed rule may represent a de fact technical barrier to trade under NAFTA that would likely be challenged in the WTO.

III.   Proposed Rule Has Serious National Security Implications

In addition to the economic and legal implications of including premium cigars cited above, there may be very real consequences for American national security. Any regulatory measures that jeopardize employment throughout much of Latin America, by impacting production, could result in adverse internal and external political climate changes. that work against American national interests, and overall economic and political stability in the region.

Again, the handmade cigar industry creates 350,000 direct jobs in the Caribbean Basin. If one considers the families reliant on the premium cigar industry for income, the number of people who would be impacted by FDA regulation of premium cigars explodes to over 1,000,000 individuals (including thousands of jobs employing Haitian farm workers in the Dominican Republic). The industry provides families with living wages, health care and education. By FDA's own account, as many as 50% of existing cigar lines may be forced to exit the marketplace as a direct result of the proposed rule. The negative impact and unintended consequences of this regulation could contribute to the type of economic instability the region has experienced in recent history.

Moreover, President Obama has announced an initiative to advance relations with Cuba. One of Cuba's best-known products – and one sure to be a major export to the United States – is premium cigars. FDA's inclusion of premiums in this rule could result in tension during this critical period and, at a minimum, sends a mixed message in its timing. It also compromises the possibility of American small businesses' benefitting from access to this important market.

The potential economic, legal, and national security implications of FDA's proposed rule are significant and have been left unanalyzed by FDA. If FDA chooses to issue a final Deeming rule, it should fully consider these issues and take that analysis into consideration when determining whether premium cigars should be included.

C.   Environmental Impact

Petitioner claims a categorical exclusion under 21 C.F.R. § 25.31.

D.   Economic Impact Statement

Petitioner will, upon request by the Commissioner, submit additional economic impact information, in accordance with 21 C.F.R. § 10.30(b).

E.   Certification

The undersigned certifies that, to the best knowledge and belief of the undersigned, this petition includes all information and views on which the petition relies, and that it includes representative data and information known to the Petitioner, which are unfavorable to the Petition.

Sincerely,

Michael E. Copperman

Michael E. Copperman
Director of Legislative and Regulatory Affairs
Cigar Rights of America
300 New Jersey Avenue, NW
Washington, DC 20001

www.ingramcontent.com/pod-product-compliance
Lightning Source LLC
Chambersburg PA
CBHW081759280526
45789CB00008B/2927